David is one of the baby boomers from parents still celebrating the end of the war. Born in Stamford in 1947, the family moved to the country when he was 11 years old to the Wooden House, described in the story, where the most impressionable period of his life was spent. Apart from a brief period in the Merchant Navy, his working life was in Financial Services.

David has dined out many times over the years on this story when it was always greeted with incredulity, humour and warmth.

To the memory of Eric and Edie.

David Bradshaw

EDIE'S LAST CHRISTMAS

AUSTIN MACAULEY PUBLISHERS™

LONDON • CAMBRIDGE • NEW YORK • SHARJAH

A CIP catalogue record for this title is available from the British Library.

ISBN 9781528919135 (Paperback)
ISBN 9781528972598 (ePub e-book)

www.austinmacauley.com

First Published (2019)
Austin Macauley Publishers Ltd
25 Canada Square
Canary Wharf
London
E14 5LQ

Thank you to my brother, John, for his kindness to his parents, despite his Victorian upbringing.

Also, to my wife, Lyn, without whose help, support and, not least, proof reading, this book might never have happened.

Eric and Edie:
Till Death Do Us Apart

As a wave from a stormy sea rushing up the beach before its energy is spent and the intensity gone, were how my emotions played out by Edie's death. The wave retreats back into the sea, just leaving the smooth sand evidence of its existence.

Relief that her ordeal, tinged with sadness for the wasted years in her later life, is over.

The strength of emotions when informed even of an expected death, followed by the acceptance of the event, may not give any visible sign on one person of what is happening inside of him.

The stormy sea almost overwhelmed me as the vertical coffin with Edie's body slumped inside precariously balanced on the top step, and I alone carried it down. Ending in a tug-o'-war between who did not want the body and the subsequent possibility of her body being returned by the undertaker to me on Christmas Eve. These events occurred in late December, 1988 and provided myself and my family with a Christmas never to be forgotten.

First, however, it is important to introduce our main characters and the events leading up to the bizarre, poignant, funny and true account that many times I have considered committing this tale to paper since this scarcely believable chain of events took place almost 30 years ago.

Chapter 1
One Fine Day

Sometime in the hot summer of 1976 on a regular visit to see my parents, when in their early 70s, I was greeted with somewhat long faces informing me that they had a serious matter to discuss with me. Eric and Edith had decided, as part of their 'Last Will and Testament', to donate their bodies to a university for medical research and to have no religious service at any funeral. I quickly established to my own relief that there was no immediate urgency about this decision, they had been mulling it over between themselves for quite some time.

I must admit that I thought it a noble gesture and willingly gave them my support. I would ensure their last wishes were carried out when the day duly arrived. They had, in fact, set up the whole process, completed all the relevant paperwork and presented it to me as a 'fait accompli'. They explained the procedure I would need to follow on the first and subsequent death and gave me a small briefcase, which I keep to this day, with all the instructions and relevant telephone numbers in. This included a copy of their written and witnessed authority at the university, which formed part of their Last Will and Testament.

It all seemed so simple and easy to put in effect, yet I had this slight difficulty; a nagging question was forming in the back of my mind. Not about their wishes, but about the procedure. However, as they were in relatively good health, the question didn't fully form and I put it down, while life for them resumed its normal pattern.

'Getting back on one's feet' is a phrase often used about someone recovering from an illness; it was often used about Edith in her declining years after numerous minor strokes. It is obviously never used about a person once deceased, but Edith defied this and gave a whole new meaning to the phrase at a very sad time, but in a humorous and moving way.

Dignity was everything to Eric, his one concession was the nickname bestowed upon him by his granddaughter, Lisa, before she could speak correctly. She was about two and a half years old at the time, the apple of his eye and more importantly, he could still see her.

He was my father, baptised Eric Frank, and Lisa's Pots. He once seemed so tall; it was both my childhood impression and an illusion created by his skeletal frame.

His love for us, his two sons and one daughter, while never expressed physically or verbally, was unquestionable. Born on 10 March 1904, he was by any standard, Victorian in his attitude, the 'stiff upper lip' and founder member of the 'hang 'em and flog 'em brigade'; his attitude on racism, gender issues and sexuality stood him somewhere to the right of Genghis Khan. He was of another generation, one that rarely admitted to or displayed affection or emotion. He was a man of few interests and fewer words.

He started his working life as a clicker in what I believe was his father's business, cutting the uppers for children's shoes from the leather waste generated by the shoe industry that was dominant in Northampton in the early 20th century. This did not last and by the age of 26, he had joined a major industrial insurance company. He spent the rest of his working life in the insurance industry collecting pennies on the clients' doorsteps of his round. By the time the main events in this narrative occurred, he had been retired for many years.

Being 'a man of few words', he was very closed about his childhood and early life. Some things we do know; he was the youngest of four and the only boy. He was apparently close to his mother, we know that he had an intense animosity towards his father and after a dispute, did not speak to him for the rest of his father's life. One anecdote that the family has, is that many years into the rift, Eric was at an insurance company dinner in a good hotel where his father, much reduced in circumstances, and in his 70s was waiting at table. Neither of them acknowledged the presence of the other and none of Eric's colleagues was aware of the identity of the ageing waiter.

None of his children: myself, my brother John, who was ten years older than me, my sister Shirley, who was fourteen years older than me, ever met any of his family. It seems his sisters all suffered from mental health problems and were all sectioned at some time in their lives. We suspect Eric felt ashamed of his sisters' problems, which may have caused him to prevent any of his children from meeting them. Both John and myself can remember Eric's occasional visit to see his youngest sister in an asylum; we were taken unwillingly, my brother in a side car and myself 10 years later in a very old car, to a distance of over 40 miles, then had to sit outside the institution for a couple of hours in winter and summer. We were never invited in and hence never met her. It was surmised by myself and my siblings, from odd snatches of things he said over the years, that Eric believed his father was the cause of the problems. We suspect abuse took place in his youth by his father, probably against his sisters. Such things were not discussed in the early 1900s, so we can only speculate about his early life.

He was, in some ways, unconventional, anti-religion and claimed not to have any belief in God. He was, however, a strong believer in spiritualism and the only reading matter in the house was *the Psychic News* and books on psychic phenomena, apart from his devotion to the *Daily Express*, which he read from cover to cover every day and believed every word of. Like many Victorians, discussions often revolved around the supernatural, ghosts and poltergeists, to which he claimed personal experience.

Chapter 2
Heath Cottage

His life with Edith was generally happy, and they were probably at their happiest when they, in their early 50s, managed to buy a house for the first time in their lives, and in 1959, moved into Heath Cottage. This was a wooden house out in the country about forty years old at the time, in need of some serious renovation and modernisation. They moved with me, the only child still in the nest aged 11, in to the house without running water, mains electricity or mains drainage. Water from a nearby spring fetched in a bucket, oil lamps at night and a midden in the garden; the bucket from which had to be buried in the garden on a weekly basis, as it was too far for the night soil men to collect it.

Cooking was courtesy of an old-fashioned range in the kitchen, and bath time once a week, whether we needed it or not, was in a scullery with an ancient copper to heat the water; fetched up by bucket from the spring and a tin bath hanging by a hook on the wall.

They set about modernising the property with great enthusiasm, but not with a great deal of knowledge. At the age of twelve, I was heavily involved in the work and thrived on it. I soon learned that my father's enthusiasm for renovation work was not matched by the skill needed to achieve the desired result.

Within a few months it was arranged for the electric company to erect several poles and wire the property to the mains supply. Eric, however, decided to wire the house himself, which nearly foreshortened his life. He was one of those men who should never have been allowed near tools, especially electrically powered ones. I witnessed him trying to wire an electric light and when he turned on the current before fitting the switch, he decided the wire was too long and cut through it with a pair of scissors. Fortunately, he was wearing a pair of Wellington boots, which insulated him from the ground, but it still blew a hole in the scissors. He obviously survived the incident which left him quite shaken and me also.

He bought an electric hedge trimmer and within a relatively short period of time, the cable had been cut by the trimmer so frequently that the cable looked more like a knotted climbing rope where it had been joined by insulation tape. However, the move to this property revitalised Edie who was enjoying the whole adventure as she saw it, and a little of her happiness rubbed off on to him.

He retired from active employment on his 65th birthday and lived until he was a few days short of his 93rd birthday.

Throughout his life, he held an unwavering love for my mum Edith, Edie as he called her. Born on 14 April 1906, she was the eldest child of seven. Her father, Archibald, was one of the characters who spent a significant period of his life in the industrial insurance industry, until he retired. He did his stint in the trenches during the First World War and survived: having been too old for early call up, he ended up among the 'past their prime' call up when the manpower for more cannon fodder was desperate. His main legacy from the war was what was then called shell shock that left him waking up shouting in the middle of the night, reliving his experiences in the trenches, for the rest of his life. Today known as Post Traumatic Stress Disorder, but during the First World War not even recognised.

Edie's mother Florence was rescued by Archie from work 'below stairs' where she was a scullery maid and they married on 18th of June 1905.

Edie spent most of her childhood helping her mother with confinements; new babies, if they were not stillborn and caring for the existing and increasing brood. Not an unusual situation for the eldest daughter at the start of the 20th century.

Her innate intelligence was never trained, never having had the opportunity of a formal education.

She told me that she used to go to school sometimes until she was 13 years old.

Edie did, however, have a natural gift in music and learned to play the violin reasonably well. It was when she was playing in one of a number of competitions she had entered, that she met Eric. He also played the violin, but with more enthusiasm than skill. He was far too shy to approach her; she, however, had spotted him, liked what she saw and took the initiative. This was something she did for the rest of her life, she would lead the way and he would follow. His nature was timid and cautious and she often had to bully him into action. This happened at its most forceful when they saw the opportunity of moving from rented accommodation to buying the wooden house. She actually threatened to divorce him if he did not buy, which was eventually done under sufferance. Once they had completed the purchase and were living in it though, he loved it and took pleasure in his attempts to improve it, with significant practical help and support from my elder brother John, who when on leave from the Marines, would spend his time working on the house.

Edie started her working life as, what was then called, a sick visitor with the same insurance company Archie, her dad, worked for. On a small 80cc motorcycle called a Coventry Eagle, she would tour the villages on her patch, visiting the claimants.

As a result of her lack of formal education and after her marriage to Eric, she spent her life in a series of mundane jobs in catering establishments or factories to assist the family budget. One of these jobs was as an usherette at the local fleapit (cinema, for the younger generation). I was too young to be left on my own, so was taken along with her to work. This meant that I got to stay up late and see all the latest horse operas, on some occasions the same one three days in a row. I don't remember minding and, at the age of about seven, I found it rather exciting.

In some ways they were an ill-matched couple: Eric very formal, serious and Victorian in every way and Edie mischievous, with a wicked sense of humour and fun-loving.

It was no surprise that they often clashed over the most mundane things. I remember quite clearly Edie coming home from the local Friday Market one spring day with some marigolds for planting in the garden. Edie had to work on the following day so had planned to plant them out in the evening when she arrived home from work.

Eric thought he would help out, so planted them for her. Her reaction, when she saw them, was not a happy one; she stormed down the garden and pulled them all up, saying that they looked like soldiers lined in rows and she wanted a flowerbed, not a military parade. It led to a full and frank exchange between them, which took some days to settle.

It was her mischief that I remember the most, particularly in the case of the virgin births. I was about 12-13 years old, loved living in the wooden house in the country and had devised a plan to utilise some of the huge garden. I wanted to breed rabbits for meat and sell them to the local butchers. So, I set about building the necessary cages and acquiring the first rabbits, several does and a buck, large New Zealand Whites. Then I carefully planned a breeding program to provide a steady but constant flow of animals, by controlling the mating dates between the buck and the does.

However, with my limited knowledge of the rabbit reproductive system, I became confused when some of the does gave birth before I had mated them. My father could not discuss such matters. Edie could shed (or rather would shed) no light on the problem, yet it continued to happen. All was revealed one day when I arrived home from school early to find Edie and a friend down the garden with the rabbits where Edie had put the buck in with a doe, and both enjoying the spectacle of the rabbits mating. Edie shamefacedly confessed the crime, but Eric never found out; he would have been horrified and deeply embarrassed about it.

Eric, with his almost skeletal frame, would describe Edie as 'a buxom lass': a problem that was growing with age. Two years younger than him, old age, deteriorating arthritic hips and an excess of shortbread biscuits, digested with the help of a new pair of well-fitting false teeth were, as the years rolled by, taking a serious toll on her health.

Chapter 3
The Light Goes Out

It was in their mid-70s when Eric's sight was beginning to fail, something he strenuously denied. They made the sad decision they had to sell the house—their last house—and move into sheltered accommodation. The phrase 'last house' was not lightly chosen because they went through a period during early retirement when they sold the cottage and moved back into town. Unable to settle, they kept moving house, financially fuelled by a housing boom. Wherever they moved to, the house/bungalow was always just what they wanted, but after about a month they began to find fault with it and within three months it was not what they wanted and they had put it on the market. At one time it seemed they were moving so frequently, I was worried I might lose touch with them between monthly visits, or even worse, it became a family joke that they would die in a removal van.

The combination of Edie's reducing mobility and Eric's gradual loss of sight forced them to consider their options on where to live and the responsibility of a house and garden. Eric was still strenuously denying that his sight was failing, until he turned his car into someone's driveway, thinking it was a turning on his usual route home, and only just managed to avoid driving into the garage door. This forced him to admit the problem with his vision and he made the necessary but hard decision to give up driving.

Eric's failing vision was the cause of the only real disagreement I had with him in his later life. Shortly before their move to sheltered accommodation he had been diagnosed with Glaucoma, he was assured by his GP (General

Practitioner) that it was a problem, but that it could be managed provided he took the prescribed medication. Treatment in the 1970s was not as sophisticated as today, and he was given a short course of oral medication and some eye drops. He was warned that the oral medication might irritate his bladder but only for the month he took it. He started the medication, found the discomfort in his bladder too great and promptly ceased taking it, along with the eye drops. He would not listen to entreaties from Edie, myself or my brother that he was putting his sight at risk, and was, shortly after, rushed into hospital with total sight loss in one eye, the sight in the other eye fading away completely over the next few years.

Fortunately, they were able to find a suitable place in the town they had lived in for the last forty years. It was a warden-controlled, self-contained flat, and they lived there for about four years. Eric's sight failed completely at the same time as Edith's mobility and general health continued to deteriorate. They soon reached a point where they needed daily help, which they found hard to come to terms with. Completely adamant about their independence and totally unaware of the increasing dirt surrounding them, Edie's mobility became so limited that it fell to Eric to maintain the running of the flat.

I vividly recall on one of my morning visits arriving with the milkman. He stood bemused outside their flat, scratching his head and pondering the liquid washing up bottle where the empty milk bottle should have been. Needless to say, I found the milk bottle empty and under the sink with the cleaning materials.

Chapter 4
Uncomfortable Bed Fellows

This was a sad period in their lives. Deteriorating health in an aged loved-one is a painful process to witness. The cruel reality of it for them was overlaid with images of the people you once knew—youthful, vital, energetic and with a mental grasp that was now obviously slipping. Life for Eric and Edie was on a continuous downhill slope. Edie reached a stage where her life revolved around food and the opening of her bowels. Her only mobility was between her bed, the toilet and the settee, with the help of Eric and a Zimmer frame. Her spirit was indomitable, convinced that although now approaching eighty and grossly overweight, she believed that the pending replacement hip operation would cure all her problems and she would soon be marching to town again to do her shopping.

Obesity and arthritis are frequent but uncomfortable bedfellows, and increase dramatically both the time and the effort required to move about. If you couple this dilemma with the preoccupation of that generation with regular bowel movement, usually aided by the liberal use of various laxatives whether necessary or not, the ongoing potential for a disaster is ever-present.

With Edie this resulted in more frequent, more rapid and messier visits to the toilet just at that time of life when her body was less able to meet the requirement for speed. Eric, while at that time still physically strong and robust, was now totally blind. He was regularly left with the job of trying to clear up the mess from one of Edie's failed loo visits, a mess he could not see but could surely smell.

The need for some help in just keeping the place clean was glaring. Many attempts to try to get them some help were made, all were rebuffed. To try an alternate way of helping, I started a process of regularly redecorating the flat as an excuse to clean up. How often can you repaint someone's bathroom before they smell a rat (excuse the pun) and realise what is going on? They would always protest violently that they were not dirty people and could manage. In the final analysis, which was the most important, a clean flat or their pride and dignity intact? This was a difficult balance to judge.

The date for Edie's replacement hip operation eventually came round, but her age, weight and general lack of fitness worked against her. She survived the surgery well, but it was only a partial success. It relieved her pain but she was never able to regain even a modest level of mobility. The weight problem was out of control by now and within days of being discharged from hospital, while struggling around the flat on crutches, she fell badly and was readmitted as an emergency for further surgery to put the damage right.

While Edie was in hospital, Eric came to stay with myself and my family. He was fit and able to manage stairs but needed a lot of guidance around the house. This was the saddest of times for Eric. He had to admit and accept that he could no longer manage to look after Edie and asked me for assistance in finding a residential care home for them. This was not easy for him to come to terms with, especially for such a self-reliant man. He was well-aware of the monumental change about to take place in their lives and their relationship in a marriage that had lasted over 50 years.

As I was living the closest to them, my brother living in London some 80 miles away, it made practical sense for me to deal with this. My sister had died just a few years ago; a traumatic event for them at a time in their lives when they were becoming less able to handle anything so awful.

With my slightly less youthful but enthusiastic innocence of the workings of the Social Services, I collided with the wall of inertia that surrounded the care of the elderly in the 1980s. Start with the obvious: Edie was back in hospital for an unspecified period, not in immediate danger but blocking a bed. So, I asked the nurse how to set about finding and funding residential care for the two of them; she suggested I had a word with the doctor. He advised me that it fell under the jurisdiction of the Department of Social Security; when approached, they told me they required a referral from a doctor before they would look into the case.

There was, however, a Social Worker's office within the hospital. I contacted her and she suggested I start looking for a suitable care home, but told me that she could only become involved if it was part of her caseload. I felt a bit like the parcel in the game that children play 'pass the parcel.' I soon discovered that finding a double billet in a residential home within 30 miles of their hometown was akin to searching for the Holy Grail. After much tripping around, looking at a variety of homes, I had no success in finding a double billet, let alone one that was suitable for them to provide the care they needed. However, I kept looking.

The issue of finding accommodation for them was becoming increasingly more pressing as the day would surely come when the hospital wanted Edie's bed. Eric was still with us during this period, which stretched to almost three months. It wasn't ever going to be possible for them both to live with us, having a young family and full-time jobs. Eric was totally blind now and Edie virtually immobile and incontinent. They needed suitable accommodation where they could be together and receive the right care.

Chapter 5
Mission Improbable

Having made no progress in the search for suitable accommodation, during the three months Edie was in hospital, the stress levels were beginning to rise. I kept Eric informed of my lack of progress, so he was aware of what was going on. Eventually, Eric and I reached an accord on how to deal with the problem; he understood that Edie needed care and I could not provide it. He also worked out that if the hospital discharged Edie into my care, they would wash their hands of the problem. The day inevitably came when the hospital wanted the bed, and the doctors at last realised Edie was in no fit state to return to her home. The hospital did try, as expected, to discharge her to me and my family. I knew, and so did Eric, that if they had succeeded in doing this, they would have soon lost interest in Eric and Edie's need for long-term care, and we would have had no assistance. Both Eric and I were adamant that this was not going to happen.

The transformation in everybody's attitude bordered on miraculous. The doctor was helpful, he wanted the bed freed and made sure the social services staff was aware of the fact, he made a formal referral. My three months of trying to avoid this situation had achieved nothing. Now, however, it was expected to be resolved at once. It was suggested by the doctor in charge of Edie's case that while we were looking for suitable accommodation for them, I should look after them at my home just as a temporary measure. This suggestion was rebuffed by Eric and myself, for the reasons stated above.

For a second time, I toured all suitable homes in the area and yet again no double billet vacancies existed, only finding two vacancies for single people. I extended the search further afield, but very few of the care homes were attractive and some you could smell stale urine before you went in. The vast majority I would not choose, but it was becoming a case of 'beggars could not be choosers'. Social Services decided they would have to split them up; only a threatened trip by me to the newspapers forestalled their plans. The potential bad publicity of forcibly splitting up a couple after over 50 years together seemed to refocus minds on keeping them together.

Eventually, a double room was found in a converted rectory, a recently registered new residential home. It was barely suitable because the room was on the first floor, with only a chairlift, and more important still, no en suite facility, though a commode was promised by the owners. At least Eric and Edie would be together, and with the aid of an ambulance, they were duly installed.

This building perched on the top of a long slope overlooking a village was owned by a farmer and his wife, a qualified nurse who lived on the premises. The complement of elderly residents varied to a maximum of around twelve.

Chapter 6
Together Again

Eric and Edie took up residence there to resume their lives together, this being the most important aspect for them. They quickly integrated into the routine of the Home, which provided the basic necessities of life to their shrinking world. It resolved some of the problems of living on their own, cooking, cleaning, dealing with utilities, and the general responsibilities of running and managing a home, but took away the independence they had been used to for 50 years. An independence they had lost long ago, but still struggled to accept that loss.

Edie regained just enough mobility with the aid of a walking frame to make it to the chairlift at lunchtime, which delivered her to the door of the dining room. She did seem to summon up superhuman strength at the sound of the dinner gong and was never late. Food was a comfort and an event that broke up the boredom of their shrinking lives and offered some social interaction. Her motivation to eat was awesome; she seemed driven by it. Eric was still robust physically but had not learned how to cope with his blindness. He tended to grope his way around the building; his sense of direction even when sighted was never good and now in new accommodation even worse.

The staircase was straight but long. I remember the first time I saw it, looking up at it and seeing it narrowing into the distance to accommodate the extremely high ceilings. This would not have created difficulty if the chairlift had not been so grindingly slow; it seemed to take an eternity to deposit a resident at the bottom and then go back up to collect the next.

I believe all the residents lived on the first floor, so a sizable gathering could always be found at the top of the chairlift at mealtimes. One got the feeling that the ones elbowed to the rear could miss out completely. For sure, before the last ones made it to the dining room, the earlier ones had finished and were taking the overworked chairlift for the ride back up, imparting their comments on the day's fare to the ones still waiting to come down.

The building, generally, was far from suitable, despite the alterations for residents of limited mobility. Corridors were narrow and extensive, with unexpected twists and turns frequently blocked with newly installed fire doors, ideal for trapping the frail and elderly with large Zimmer frames.

Edie was Eric's eyes, and despite her deteriorating health, she helped him learn the layout of the building. Sadly, though, she fairly quickly had some minor strokes which left her mental faculties slowing along with her physical ones. Life consisted of three daily trips to the dining room with Eric's help and a reinforced Zimmer frame. The time spent eating and travelling took up a significant part of their day, I had to be cognisant of the mealtimes, as nothing interrupted the process and visitors had to wait. The remainder of the day was often spent watching television interspersed with desperate attempts by Edie, with Pot's help, to reach the commode, not always successfully.

The owner installed an en suite toilet in a cupboard in their room. The idea was a noble one but the toilet was now some feet farther away than the commode had been from the bed. The extra distance and a sliding door turned a minor problem of not always getting there in time into a bigger disaster.

Just prior to the installation of the en suite toilet, two incidents occurred on consecutive days that must have set alarm bells ringing. This almost certainly prompted the owner into action to provide toilet facilities in their room. I suspect it also led the owners to believe that my parents were the residents from hell to look after.

This particular morning, after breakfast, Edie had decided to visit her new friend, Marjorie, who lived in the neighbouring room, for a chat. Edie limped through with her Zimmer frame into Marjorie's room. Marjorie was a relatively new resident, somewhat more mobile than Edie. Any movement for Edie was always an effort, but she managed to negotiate the two doors to access Marjorie's room and went in.

However, as she reached a chair, she caught the leg of the Zimmer frame in the television cable, lost her balance and landed in a heap on the floor with the television. Nothing was broken but the shock triggered a bowel movement and the resulting mess took some time to clear up, which upset poor Marjorie. Some staff soon whisked Edie back to her room, cleaned her up and allowed her to recover on her bed, while Marjorie's room was cleaned and refreshed. The only lasting damage was to Edie's dignity and Marjorie's television set.

On the following morning, the second incident occurred. It was Eric's lifelong duty as he saw it to look after Edie, and to this end he always tried to clear up any mess she had made. Always an early riser at 5 am, it became Eric's routine to empty the commode by groping his way, carrying the full bucket from the commode to the communal bathroom/toilet. This was some distance down the corridor through a couple of fire doors and a left turn.

The morning after Edie's mishap, Eric set off with a full commode bucket to the toilet, as usual feeling his way along the walls only to turn the wrong way outside the bedroom and walk into Marjorie's room carrying the commode bucket. I guessed perhaps her door was ajar so he followed the line of wall. Marjorie awoke to see what she thought was a strange man staggering around her bedroom at 5 am in the morning carrying a bucket of human excrement. She screamed, and he dropped the bucket, spilling the contents. The residents were woken by the noise and the resulting mess took somewhat longer to clear up.

These two episodes were relayed to me by Edie on my visit the next day. She concluded in all innocence 'I don't think Marjorie likes me anymore.'

Neither Eric nor Edie ever really complained about their lot, but Edie did want a comfortable chair from which she could watch the television. There was an upright dining chair in the room, but nothing you could relax on, except the bed. She asked me to help her buy one, so with family in tow, I took her out in a wheelchair, with Eric on my arm, to the local town in search of said chair. It was a good opportunity for them to see their grandchildren and to have a trip out. We found a furniture store in the local town that had, what appeared to be, a reclining chair which might fit the bill. We assisted Edie out of the wheelchair and, with some strong help, ensconced her in the chair. She said it was comfortable and she really liked it, the shop assistant explained how it reclined and stretched it out until she was almost lying down. At this point, her enthusiasm was obvious to all, the shop assistant thought he had made a sale and we were on the point of purchase. This was before the days that these chairs were electrically driven. At this moment, Edie asked about a mysterious button and pressed it. Driven by a very powerful spring which returned the chair into upright position, folding Edie into it. It had happened so quickly that Edie was almost in shock and it took some help to prize her out. That was definitely not what she wanted, and we gave up the idea of a reclining chair.

Little was I to know this was to be the last time she would ever go out.

My visits usually followed a routine, but on one occasion I went at a different time and walked in to a bemusing situation; it was early afternoon on 14 December 1988 and Edie was in amazing form. It was as if she had become rejuvenated and was sporting a crop of bright orange hair that the visiting hairdresser had dyed that morning. She was sitting upright on a stool, which was in itself surprising, animated and displaying an energy I had not seen in years.

She could not wait to tell me her news. My brother, 10 years older than me and now in his early fifties, had rung to say he had—or rather his wife, who is some years younger than him, had just given birth to their first child. The baby was going to be named Marianne, she was but a few days old and her mother had been discharged from hospital that day with the new baby. My brother's call was to tell them about Marianne and tell them that he would be bringing her to see them very soon.

During the conversation, Marianne cried out and Edie heard her little voice. Edie was very moved by this and told everyone within earshot many times. I almost believed she was recovering some of her old zest. Sadly, it was not to be, she never saw Marianne, and I did not see Edie alive again.

Chapter 7
Some Phone Call

While it is difficult to remember the exact timescales of events that occurred nearly 30 years ago, the events themselves stick in my mind as if it was yesterday. Eric and Edie had been residents together of the care home, probably one of the worst imaginable, for about two years when the following incredible sequence of events occurred:

It was a Friday evening, ten days before Christmas 1988, just approaching 9 pm, when the telephone rang in my home.

I answered it, there was a long pause before the owner of the care home introduced herself. I then had a very bizarre conversation with her. She said they had a problem. A silence followed while I waited for her to continue. She didn't, so I eventually asked, "Is it my mum again?"

Another long pause ensued before she said, "Yes."

I said, "Oh, has she had another stroke?"

I took the following silence as an affirmative. "This must be the fifth or sixth. Is she at the Home or has she gone to hospital?"

There was another long pause before she replied, "No, she is still at the Home."

"Well, obviously my dad is with her. Has the doctor been called?" I asked.

Another long pause before she replied, "Yes, yes, he visited and has now gone."

I waited for her to continue. After a long pause when it became obvious she wasn't going to, I asked, "What did he say?" There was another long pause so I asked if it was serious.

She said, "Yes."

It was now gradually dawning on me how serious this was.

"Is she dead?" I asked.

"Yes," she replied.

The protracted nature of the news prepared me for this, though I doubt it was deliberate on her part. It was no real surprise and I admit to feeling some relief, Edie was free from pain and the mounting indignities in her life.

I told her I would come straightaway and asked her how my dad was.

Now the information she had had such difficulty imparting was finally out; she seemed to relax and open up. She told me Eric was with Edie when she died and he is currently downstairs in the kitchen in front of a good fire with a couple of the other residents. The Home was a converted rectory with a large kitchen. I explained it would take me about 35 minutes to get there and I was on my way. I rang off, broke the news to my family and left.

I gathered up their 'Will Case' which held instructions for what to do in the event of their deaths. I cannot claim a premonition but I had been looking at it recently to remind myself of the practical after-death procedure of donating one's body to medical science.

I arrived about 10 pm and found Dad seated by a warm fire in the rectory kitchen in the company of a couple of other residents. He was naturally upset and told me briefly how she had died; she had been propped up in bed watching television when she said that she had a severe pain in her lower back. She asked him to gently rub it for her and while he was massaging her back, she laid back and died.

He said she did not appear to suffer and it happened quickly. He said that although he could not see her, he knew she was dead.

I spent some time with him, then told him I must sort out the arrangements for Mum's body to be collected. He understood and asked me to ensure her wishes were fulfilled. I left him still sitting by the fire with a replenished mug of hot tea in his hand, promising I would return as soon as I had finished what I needed to do.

I remember thinking to myself how much of a shock it must have been for him. He was 84 years old himself and had been with Edie for over 50 years. I can't say 'never a cross' word passed between them, but they jogged along. He looked very tired and weary; I wanted to see if I could get him to bed when I had sorted things out. I hoped he'd sleep and then I could come and see him again the next day.

The husband of the owner of the Home cornered me as I left Eric. Out of Eric's earshot, he told me I needed to arrange for the body to be moved tonight, then told me he had requested the local undertaker to handle the arrangements and that the undertaker (singular) was waiting outside for my instructions to come in to collect Edie. I suspected some pecuniary arrangement was in place between them but had other more pressing matters to deal with. There was an immediate issue I needed to explain to him that my parents had donated their bodies to a university for medical research. There was a strict procedure that needed following. I had an exclusive telephone number to ring where the arrangements would be taken over and the body collected by the university's undertaker.

Everything else would have to wait, I now needed to focus on what I had to do.

I also needed a few minutes alone with Edie to say goodbye; there was not going to be a funeral, the body would soon be whisked away, I thought, to be used by the medical students and, when the university had finished with it, they would, as agreed, dispose of the remains without referring back to the relatives. There wasn't going to be another opportunity for me to say my own goodbye.

Chapter 8
Not the Send-Off Anticipated

As I walked into Eric and Edie's room, I noticed an empty coffin propped up against the wall. Then I saw Mum lying on the bed. Seeing her engendered a wave of feelings to flood through me. Relief for her, sadness, missing her already, and some shock. I wanted to remember the good times when she was younger—full of life, energetic, tireless, optimistic, tactless, but with a heart of gold.

Now her life was over and I had to fulfil my promise and concentrate on what I had to do. So, I sat on the chair beside the bed, told her what I was going to do and that she could listen in.

The first thing to do was to ring the dedicated telephone number to organize collection of the body. I found it in the 'Will' case and noticed the relevant correspondence was dated 1976. It was now 12 years since that hot summer's day when they'd told me their wishes.

The correspondence stated that the number was open 24 hours a day and that the university would organize collection of the body, provided there was a preliminary death certificate issued by a doctor. The doctor had left this with the homeowner who had given it to me on my arrival.

Fortunately, there was a telephone in the room, so I sat next to Edie and rang the number, confident that despite it being almost 11 o'clock on a Friday night, only ten days before Christmas, all would be well. I rang the number. It rang and rang and rang. In the absence of an alternative option, I let it ring. It must have been ringing for almost ten minutes when it was answered. A happy drunken voice on the end of the phone said, "Come to the party!" I could hear Jingle Bells in the background and laughter echoed round the bedroom. I tried to explain that my mother had just died and that this was the number I had to ring to arrange collection of the body. The voice replied, "Bring her to the party, no one will mind."

It eventually transpired that this was no longer the correct number to ring. This was now the number for the student halls and they were having their Christmas party; everyone was welcome, dead or alive.

I knew that if Edie had heard this conversation, she would have laughed at the whole farce. I persevered with the drunken student, not knowing what else to do. He eventually sobered up enough to realize the gravity of the situation and suggested I ring the Vice Principal's office to sort it out, and gave me his number.

By this time, I was feeling slightly desperate, so I rang the number the student had given me. It was answered quickly and crossly by, I assumed, the Vice Principal who curtly asked who was ringing him at this time on a Friday night. He told me he was going out to a function and running very late, which seemed odd at so late an hour, well after 11 pm.

I tried to explain my situation but he was so cross that he didn't want to hear. Our voices rose higher and a frank exchange took place. I told him that if he didn't listen, I would bring the body over in the car and deliver it to him personally. One cannot know, but I suspected at this point it finally dawned on him that this was not a student prank. He calmed down and we both apologized.

After I recapped the situation, he became far more constructive; he thought for a minute or so, then suggested I let the local undertaker take the body and contact the university's undertaker (whose name he quickly provided) at the first opportunity, who would collect the body from its temporary home and pay for the relevant storage. This released the pressure on me and gave me, or so I thought, a way to resolve the immediate problem. I thought Edie, apart from enjoying the joke, would be satisfied with the way things were going so far.

Now I faced the task of getting Edie's body into the coffin. It was made of flimsy plastic with a clip-on lid and did not look or feel sturdy enough to carry anything substantial. I called the undertaker who was still waiting to take the body and to explain the situation to him. He took a while to get upstairs, being quite elderly himself, and arrived alone and breathless; I found myself wondering if he was one of the residents who had wandered in! He told me he was 82 years of age and could not lift much weight. His two sons who ran the business now were at a Christmas party, so he'd come himself and brought over the wagon and their plastic carrying coffin. I explained the situation and he agreed to store the body until it was collected.

Edie must have weighed over 13 stone; I now understand the meaning of the phrase 'dead weight'. There was no way the two of us could lift her into the coffin; help was required. I ran down and asked the homeowner's husband to help us. This request was received with some obvious reluctance but I pointed out that if he wanted the body moved tonight he needed to help and he grudgingly agreed.

The undertaker provided two lifting straps. I wrestled them under Edie's body as she was lying on her back and spaced them at a suitable spread to support her. I stood one side, the homeowner's husband stood the other and the aged undertaker took the feet. We took her weight and gently manoeuvred her into the flimsy plastic coffin, I placed the lid on and clipped it shut. By the time I looked up, the homeowner's husband had disappeared never to be seen again, leaving myself and the undertaker to move the coffin from the upstairs room to the hearse outside. In the absence of finding alternate help, and with the undertaker's assistance, we worked out a strategy for the first part of the journey on our own.

The undertaker agreed he could manage the foot end of the coffin if I would take the heavy end, so off we set.

I discovered a body is easier to carry in a coffin; you have something fixed to lift it by, something solid to grip and get your arms under. However, trying to navigate a way through winding corridors with heavy-duty fire doors at intervals blocking one's way, while walking backwards carrying the heavy end of a weighty coffin, was a challenge.

I somehow managed to shoulder-open the doors and keep the process moving until we eventually arrived at the top of the staircase. This very old building had very high ceilings and a long straight narrow staircase with the slowest chairlift I had ever encountered for the residents, and no lift. The undertaker who was already breathing heavily said he could not assist with the coffin on the staircase, it was just too heavy and he wasn't stable enough on his feet.

We laid the coffin on the landing floor and I looked at the problem. A long narrow staircase, no alternative way down, a rickety chairlift that partially blocked the stairs and a very heavy coffin with one able-bodied person to lift it down. The owner's husband was still hiding somewhere, so it was just me.

I considered sliding it down but was not confident that I could stop it escaping from me and landing at speed at the bottom. I also considered walking backwards, carrying the heavy end of the coffin and bumping the foot end down one step at a time, but was certain the box was too flimsy to withstand the battering.

The next option was the chairlift, but again I would have to walk backwards down the stairs, with the speed of descent controlled by the moving chair, while balancing the coffin across the chair. I thought this might, just as easily as the other options, result in a tangle of broken plastic and bodies (mine and Edie's) at the bottom.

Getting Mum out of the coffin and strapping her into the chairlift became a serious consideration, but was as full of potential disaster as all the others. Abandoning the coffin and leaving it there until help arrived seemed like breaking my promise to her and would upset Eric even more. Poor blind Eric would have to navigate around his beloved Edie in the box on his way to the room.

Finally, I decided the only way was to carry the coffin down myself. I was young and strong then and knew I could do it. To achieve this, I stood the coffin up on its narrow end and, as I did so, I heard Edie slump down inside. I remember thinking that I was getting my old mum back onto her feet for the last time. I was also working out that at least it helped to lower the centre of gravity, making the coffin easier to balance on the way down.

Cuddling the coffin close to my body, I could by bracing myself back against the wall, lift it down one step at a time, while keeping it balanced upright. So off I set, one step at a time, literally heaving it down to the next step, regaining my precarious balance each time, as well as catching my breath, then again bracing myself against the wall for the next lift, and repeating the process for the next step.

I was only a few steps in to this process when one of the elderly residents appeared at the bottom of the stairs, saying she wanted to come up to go to bed and needed to use the chairlift to get up the stairs. The stairs were only of a normal house width and there was no way the chairlift could be used while I was blocking the stairs. She stood on the bottom step asking what I was doing. While still bracing myself against the wall, I stopped lifting and persuaded the lady to leave until I had completed the descent, very aware that if I dropped the box, we could possibly need two coffins. Finally, she walked back into the room from which she had come, allowing me to continue with my task.

I thought it would never end. I also remember thinking, as I gradually worked the coffin to the bottom, that Edie would have laughed at the whole escapade and that she also had a last cuddle with her youngest boy. She had a wicked and unconstrained sense of humour and I know she would have appreciated the comedy of it all.

Only once did I almost lose my balance and take the quick way down. I eventually arrived at the last step and, heaving a sigh of relief, I laid the coffin flat.

The undertaker walked down the stairs and joined me at the bottom, he helped me carry the coffin to the gurney and lifted it on, walked it out to the hearse and slid it in. I had already explained to him that another firm would collect

Edie's body, probably on Monday, and pay him for his services.

It was at this point he informed me that they were only a small company and had no cold storage facilities. Panic overrode any relief I was feeling at having sorted out things thus far. What do I do now? How long before a body starts to decompose? How fresh does it need to be for the students? Will the university still accept it? The image of a decomposing corpse being delivered to the university was not one I wished to contemplate.

The undertaker himself, however, came to the rescue, suggesting that as it was December and cold, if not freezing, the weather would keep her as cold as any storage facility over the weekend. So, as my panic level subsided, I watched him drive off with my dear old mum, this being the last time I would see her.

Chapter 9
Life Goes On

Now to spend some time with Dad.

As I returned to the kitchen, I could see he was exhausted and distraught, still sitting in front of the fire. He asked me if everything was sorted and I told him all was fine and that things had gone off smoothly. It was now about 2 am, and so after a short while, I helped him upstairs to his bed and he quickly fell asleep.

As I drove home, I started reflecting on the events and how they had all unravelled. I felt relief that it was all sorted out and wondered what needed to be done next. First, I needed to register the death with the Births, Deaths and Marriages office. I would nip into Peterborough on Monday and deal with that.

Second, I needed to contact the university's funeral parlour, to confirm that they were aware and that they needed to collect the body as soon as possible.

I wanted to see Eric again tomorrow, now today, and spend some time with him. Then I needed to sort out Edie's finances, stop her pension and benefits, and renegotiate the payment to the Home. The finances I knew could wait, but the adrenalin I'd been running on was still working, so my mind would not shut off.

But most important of all, I needed to get some sleep. It was about 3 am by the time I got home and I felt physically, mentally and emotionally drained.

The whole event felt surreal, made doubly difficult by not being able to tell Dad anything about the problems I had encountered. I knew he would rest easy believing I had sorted it all without any difficulty and that Edie was on her way. They were so different; she would have enjoyed the craziness of the whole episode, in fact if I believed in an afterlife, I'd say she planned it (she sure had the mischief in her). Eric, though, would have been appalled. He would have been too upset by every aspect of what happened that night for me to consider telling him even the smallest part of it.

If only I had known on my drive home that my problems were still in their early stages.

Saturday

After some sleep, I was able to focus more easily on the night's events. They seemed even more bizarre in retrospect than at the time. I knew I'd have Mum's permission for this to be a story to dine out on in the future, but for the moment I had to concentrate on what needed to be done in the immediate.

I cannot say I was grief-stricken, I was sad for my dad but I was glad Edie's suffering was over and I still felt overwhelmingly relieved.

I contacted my brother, John, first thing Saturday to tell him Edie had died and updated him on the night's events, not least the necessity of not telling Eric what had passed or the problems I was still encountering, and asked him if he could visit him on Sunday, which he did. In fact, he collected Eric and took him back to his home to stay for Christmas.

John and I had an understanding over the years. I lived the closest and so would make the regular visits to see Eric and Edie and look after their routine stuff, including their finances, and he would give them a break from the residential home by taking them back to his house for a week's holiday, from time to time.

I took the family over to see their Pots on Saturday morning and to provide him with some distraction and comfort. He was remarkably calm, with feelings akin to my own; he had witnessed Edie's problems over the years and her increasing distress.

There was nothing practical I could do on Saturday or Sunday as all the places I needed to contact were closed.

Monday

Now, with Eric safely ensconced at my brother's, I could start making phone calls. Edie's body needed collecting as a matter of urgency so I started there. I phoned the university's undertakers and explained the situation. They confirmed they would collect Edie from her temporary resting place and reimburse the current undertakers for their services. I subsequently discovered that they collected Edie that very day.

They also provided me with an urgent list of requirements that had to be met before the university would accept the body and stressed the urgency by saying it all had to be completed before Christmas.

The list and the tight time scale felt daunting. They needed written confirmation that the body was free from contagious diseases, the registered death certificate and a copy of her Last Will and Testament confirming this action represented her last wishes. I was getting the impression that the university did not wish to be accused of following in the footsteps Burke and Hare, the notorious body snatchers of the early 1820s.

Early afternoon and I was now free from my normal job to visit the office of Births, Deaths, and Marriages office to register Edie's death in my local town of Peterborough, expecting the process to be straightforward.

How wrong could I have been!

The assistant behind the counter asked if she could help me. I replied that I wished to register the death of my mother that had taken place the previous Friday night. I was informed by her that it was a straightforward procedure, they just needed to confirm that I was next-of-kin and to see the Certificate of Death provided by the attending doctor. No problem, I had the relevant papers to hand ready.

Then I was told that there was a problem, that a death must be registered in the district in which it took place. That not being Peterborough, this death could not be registered at this office. I needed to go to the office in the district in which she had died, a small town about 25 miles away. She added that it was only a part-time office, open just one afternoon a week on a Monday. It was suggested I make an appointment for the following Monday.

I pointed out that it would be Boxing Day and therefore unlikely to open. They, while being very sympathetic, could not help me resolve my dilemma.

I explained the situation to them and the urgency I faced in resolving it, not least that if the information was not provided within the time scales laid down, the body would be returned to me for burial.

I asked if I could use their phone to ring the other registry office. They were happy to oblige.

The following is a summary of the conversation that ensued:

"Is that the registry office?"

"Yes, can I help you?"

"I need to register my mother's death. I live in Peterborough but am informed that the death has to be registered in the district in which she died, this being yours. Could I make an appointment for later today or tomorrow?"

"I'm sorry but we are closing now, we only open one afternoon a week and that is Monday. Next Monday is the earliest we could see you."

"Next Monday is Boxing Day!"

My panic level was starting to rise.

"Look, there is a real problem here: she died on December 16, today is 19. Next Monday is December 26, Boxing Day. I doubt even you will be open on that day, so are you suggesting I delay registering the death until after the holiday?"

I tried to calmly explain my problem but was confronted with a wall of resistance.

"I know it is not your fault, but I need to solve the problem before my mother's body decomposes, and leaving it until next year could increase that risk."

I asked them to stay at the office and keep it open while I drive over straightaway; it would take me a little over half an hour.

After much persuasion, they finally agreed and awaited my arrival. I drove furiously to get there ASAP. I felt under enormous time pressure. Visions of Mum celebrating Christmas with the family from a coffin in the lounge did not thrill me.

On arrival at the registry office, the process was straightforward, one of providing the required information and an exchange of the doctor's death certificate for a formal one registering the death. By the time this was completed, it was too late for me to undertake (excuse the pun) the next tasks, firstly, her GP's written confirmation that she had no contagious diseases and secondly, a copy of Edie's Will.

By the time I arrived home to take copies and write the relevant letters, it was too late to action anything; it would have to wait until the next day.

Tuesday

While seeming to find pitfalls in every step, I thought I had overcome them. In order to 'belt and brace' the situation, I decided to ring the university to inform them of the stage I was at and ensure they were aware that there was a body on its way.

What a surprise—no one I spoke to had any idea that a body was coming! They stated that they would require all the paperwork, insisting they would need several days to process it upon receipt before the body would be accepted.

My stress levels started to rise again as I rang the GP's surgery and elicited that he was not in until tomorrow and for me to ring back then, when he would talk to me. Tomorrow was Wednesday, Friday was the last working day before Christmas and how much would I get done on Friday, who would even be interested?

In the hope that I could meet the university's deadline, I posted what paperwork I could to the university, saying the rest would follow as soon as possible.

Wednesday

Things got worse. The university's undertakers rang to say they did not think there was time to process the necessary forms, so they had agreed with the university to return Edie's body for a normal burial. I said that was not acceptable and reminded them that the university had been keen to accept the body when the original paperwork was set up, and it was not reasonable to refuse it at this stage because she died on an inconvenient date for them. I refused to provide an address or firm of undertakers to whom they could deliver the body. Then I informed them that they would receive all the relevant forms within the next couple of days.

It felt like a Mexican standoff. I was not prepared to accept the return of the body because the date of Edie's death interfered with their Christmas celebrations. I felt a duty to fulfil Edie's and Eric's wishes in this matter. It obviously put the undertakers, as the go-between for the university and myself, in a very difficult position, but it was also obvious they were not going to concede. The conversation came to an uncompromising end.

I realized that I needed to perform a juggling act. On one hand, trying to get all the paperwork together ASAP and on the other, to delay any actions aimed at returning Edie to me. I imagined Edie having a good laugh at what was turning into a Pythonesque sketch.

I left instructions with my wife that if the phone rang and there was the slightest suspicion that it was the undertakers, she did not understand English.

At last I spoke to Edie's GP, a very laid-back man who told me to send him the Death Certificate, which he would return in due course, along with the relevant documentation for the university. The implication was that he would get around to it, probably in the New Year. I pressed my case, saying the body was in limbo until this documentation was issued and that a tug-of-war in reverse was in process over the body, until the paperwork was completed and was in the relevant hands. He said to post him the Death Certificate and he would send the form straight back. Today was Wednesday, no time for the Christmas post to work, so I told him I would deliver the Death Certificate personally to his surgery today and hoped that he could let me have the signed certificate straight away. He pointed out, not unreasonably, that he had a lot of live patients in his surgery who needed his services more than Edie did and that he would be making house calls for the rest of the day, but would send it to me as soon as he could.

Another 25-mile drive to the doctor's surgery to deliver the papers, but at least the papers were now in his hands. There was nothing else I could do.

I rang the university to see if they had received the papers I had sent yesterday. They seemed to know nothing at all about it, let alone sending the body back. Different departments perhaps, so I agreed to fax them copies over today so at least they could start work while the Christmas post ground slowly to its delivery stage and the original papers actually arrived.

Another trip out, this time to the town library to find a fax machine, still rare in 1988, where I faxed copies of the paperwork I had already posted.

Thursday

No form from the GP in the morning post. I felt a little bluff was in order. So I rang the undertakers to tell them I had sent off all the paperwork to the university and the ball was now in their court. They said the body needed to be returned as it was too late for the paperwork to be processed. I said no and that was their problem. I left them with a distinct impression, though somewhat less than truthful, that we were away for Christmas and that we were going today. I reasoned that there was no one to whom they could return a body they

47

did not want. I intended to fulfil Edie's wishes and would not be put off by either the university's or the undertaker's unwillingness to do their job because it was Christmas. It had been agreed that her body would go for research and the fact that, from their point of view, she died at an inconvenient time was not going to stop it from happening.

I spoke to Eric on the phone—he was at my brother's house—to see how he was and to settle his mind that everything was going as planned, and that there were no problems in executing Edie's wishes. He was remarkably calm and accepting of what had occurred. He was uplifted by meeting Marianne for the first time, still only days old.

Friday

The form came from the GP, hurrah! I phoned the university to inform them I had the last bit of paper they required. They were not helpful, no one was there who knew anything about it but they did restate the now familiar script that they would require the correct paperwork in their hands before they would accept the body. I decided to fax it to them, putting the original in the post, then keeping a low profile and see what happens. I reasoned that the staff would be preoccupied with Christmas and, in fact, most of them at both the undertakers and the university would not be there to deal with it and that nothing would happen until after the Christmas period, when they were back at work. Poor old Mum would have been languishing quietly for a couple weeks by then and their ownership of her body would be de facto anyway.

Saturday

It felt a strange way to say good-bye to one's mum: the urgency of the situation in the immediate when boxing her body and carrying the coffin, then the subsequent ducking, weaving and rushing about to meet an artificial deadline set by the organisation receiving the gifted body because it coincided with Christmas.

This left me with a strange mixture of emotions. These were naturally coloured by many things, memories of the dynamic person she had been in her younger years, her lack of natural tact and an ability to say the wrong thing without realising it. But the strongest memory revolves around her unconstrained sense of humour; I just know she would have laughed at the pantomime she put me through. I still believe that to donate one's body for medical research is one of the greatest, most precious gifts anyone can make, and I sincerely hope that no one else has to jump through the hoops that I did to ensure such a gift was received.

This all felt such a relief, I could spend a day with my family doing normal things like Christmas shopping; safe in the knowledge that no one was in to answer the phone and that it was unlikely the undertakers would return the body without prior notice or knowing where to deliver it. I had nightmares for weeks of arriving home and finding the coffin stacked up against the outside wall next to the front door with Mum still inside.

She was, we assume, kept by the university as we heard no more from any of the parties involved.

Chapter 10
Home Alone

Eric's life at the Home continued alone. It was not a good place and he asked me to see if he could move to a more suitable residential home. I contacted the Royal National Institute for the Blind who put me in touch with a home for visually impaired people in Leicester, which I visited, liked and thought suitable for him. He had never come to terms with his blindness and the help they could offer him was exactly what he needed. They agreed to offer him a place as soon as one became available but could obviously not put a time scale on it. They had about forty residents, most of whom were elderly, so I reasoned it should not be too long.

In fact, his life did not continue alone for very long. Within a couple of weeks, they had moved an elderly and very sick man into his room to share with him, without consulting Eric or any real consideration for the new resident's condition. The new roommate was bedridden, asthmatic and approaching 90 years of age. He warranted nursing care, not residential home care, although I think the dividing line between the two was more blurred in those days and almost any care home that would take someone would suffice to free up a hospital bed.

His care needs were greater than the Home could or would provide and it left Eric picking up some of the inevitable problems of a bedridden patient. A simple thing like a drink of water in the night was beyond the roommate's ability but many a time Eric would get up and help. Without Edie's eyes to direct him, he would stumble across the room, groping for the glass of water to help his roommate quench his thirst.

Eric frequently used to call down for help, which meant groping his way out on to the landing and shouting over the banister rail until somebody came. It did not take long before Eric was branded a troublemaker, calling down for help at the slightest of things.

On one of my regular visits, he told me of his woes and that he was desperate to move. I could only reassure him that he was just waiting for the first vacancy in the Home in Leicester.

He had recently had a heated argument with the owners about the roommate not getting enough care. They told Eric he was overreacting by indulging the man's every whim, one of which, Eric pointed out, was listening to him choking with an asthma attack. Eric told me that that same evening he tasted something unpleasant in his evening drink and suspecting it was drugged, he told the staff who denied it, so he threw it on the floor. To my eternal shame, I doubted him, I just could not believe that the owners would do such a dreadful thing. It turned out he was correct.

One evening, unknown to Eric or any of the other residents, the owners had decided to attend a late-night function. As there was no other live-in staff, they hired an elderly, retired matron to sit in while they were out to comply with the care home regulations.

She apparently found herself a quiet room in the attic with a comfortable couch and promptly settled down to sleep, it was subsequently suspected with the aid of a chemical cosh. Around midnight, Eric's roommate had a severe asthma attack and Eric was frightened he would choke to death as he could not breathe. Eric went out on to the landing and shouted for help, managing to wake the other residents. No staff came. After about half an hour of trying desperately to get help and with the roommate still choking, he decided to use the phone in his room to ring the police.

The police and an ambulance arrived very quickly and found Eric who by now was frantic with worry. He led them to his room where the medics sorted out the choking roommate. The police then undertook a search of the building but were unable to find any staff. By this time, it was the early hours of the morning and the owners returned from their revelry to be greeted by the police who wanted to know why nobody was manning the fort. They said somebody was looking after the place and set out to look for her, eventually finding her sleeping soundly in a small attic room, totally oblivious of the commotion going on below.

During Eric's interview with the police about this incident, he told them of his suspicion that he was being poisoned by the taste of his late-night drink. To their credit, the police took this accusation seriously and interviewed all the staff, one of whom admitted that Eric was correct and that he was being drugged at night in his last hot drink to knock him out. Eric was asked by the police if he wanted to press charges against the owners of the Home. He declined to do so.

Everyone was left unhappy with the outcome, Eric's branding as a troublemaker was reinforced, the residents who had all been woken up either by Eric's shouting or the police searching their rooms, the police were far from happy with the result, and of course the owners were the unhappiest of all. This left Eric in an untenable position as a resident in this Home.

Fortunately, within days, he was offered a place in the RNIB home in Leicester, and I moved him in immediately, much to everyone's relief. A dark, sad period of his life was over.

Chapter 11
From Bad to Good

Eric quickly settled into his new home. It was a caring environment, ideally suited to his temperament and his inability to cope with his blindness. The kindness of the staff and their understanding of his difficulties caused by the onset of blindness late in life helped lift him from his sadness.

By the time Eric was moved to his new home, his and Edie's limited capital from the sale of their last house was gone, having been used to meet the shortfall between their income and their fees. Now there was another shortfall but no capital to meet it.

I approached his last employer who came to the rescue by subsidising his financial shortfall until his death.

I visited Eric on alternative Saturdays when we would either go for a drive in the car or a walk in the local park. I used to try to draw him out to glean more information about his early life. Very little was forthcoming, though I asked him about his experience during the war when he was called up late, already 40 years of age. He said he did not really enjoy his time as a trainee mechanic in the RAF (Royal Air Force). He lived in a Nissan hut and his colleagues, apparently, did not like it when he played his violin! I had to confirm that he actually took his violin with him when he went off to war.

Eric was a taciturn man by nature, but during his later years, he would be easily moved to laughter by his sons' gentle banter and teasing when John and I saw him together. He loved to be reminded about some of the funny and amusing incidents he was party to when we were all much younger.

When I asked him once what was the first car he remembered seeing, he told me it was in the street opposite where he lived as a child. From his bedroom window—this would be about 1911 or 1912 as far as I could judge, he saw an open-top car, parked in the street opposite, facing down the hill away from him, next to a gas lamppost. A man came out of the house adjacent to the car, wearing a dress suit and bow tie, from what would have been a house in the better part of the town in the early 1900s. The man was obviously of some importance, clearly very drunk and staggered to the lamppost, swung around it a couple of times and collapsed in a heap next to his car. A passing policeman on his beat arrived at the scene, picked the drunken form off the pavement, brushed him down, helped him into his car, cranked it for him and sent him on his way. Eric said I don't suppose that would happen today.

Here, he spent the last ten years of his life in this good and kind environment, where all his needs were met in as caring a way as possible.

The care home held the information relating to his last wishes, about his body going to medical research, so that when he eventually died, his body was collected by the university undertakers, it was however refused by the university for medical reasons. Eric was returned to our care, and we had a small, non-religious funeral with his two sons watching his coffin disappear behind the curtain to the sound of Eric's favourite music; Beethoven's violin Concerto.